By David Ignatow

POEMS

THE GENTLE WEIGHT LIFTER

SAY PARDON

FIGURES OF THE HUMAN

RESCUE THE DEAD

SELECTED POEMS

POEMS 1934–69

THE NOTEBOOKS OF DAVID IGNATOW

FACING THE TREE

Facing the Tree

Facing the Tree

New Poems by

DAVID IGNATOW

An Atlantic Monthly Press Book

LITTLE, BROWN AND COMPANY • BOSTON • TORONTO

FIRST EDITION

T 02/75

LIBRARY OF CONGRESS CATALOGING IN PUBLICATION DATA

Ignatow, David, 1914–
    Facing the tree.

    "An Atlantic Monthly Press book."
    I. Title.
PS3517.G53F3   811'.5'4   74-22439
ISBN 0-316-41490-5
ISBN 0-316-41491-3 pbk.

ATLANTIC—LITTLE, BROWN BOOKS
ARE PUBLISHED BY
LITTLE, BROWN AND COMPANY
IN ASSOCIATION WITH
THE ATLANTIC MONTHLY PRESS

*Published simultaneously in Canada
by Little, Brown & Company (Canada) Limited*

PRINTED IN THE UNITED STATES OF AMERICA

To Nicanor Parra,
Wherever he is
Whatever he must do
In the service
of his poetry

Some of these poems have been previously published by *Abraxas*, *American Poetry Review* ("Letter to a Friend," "My Enemies," "Talking to Myself," "Each Day," "A Moral Tale," which appeared as "In Adversity"), *Antaeus* ("Autumn"), *Arts in Society*, *The Atlantic* ("Reading the Headlines"), *Boundary II*, *Centennial Review*, *Changes*, *Chicago Tribune*, *Choice*, *Columbia Forum*, *Crazy Horse*, *Dacotah Territory*, *Equal Time*, *Field*, *Granite*, *Hawaii Literary Review*, *Kayak*, *Mill Mountain Review*, *Modern Poetry Studies*, *Mouth*, *The Nation*, *New Letters*, *The New York Quarterly*, *The New York Times*, *Occasional Papers #9* of Kent State University, *The Ohio Review*, *Organ*, *Poetry* ("I'm Here," which appeared as "Here I Am," "In This Dream"), *Rapport*, *Seneca Review*, *Shankpainter Ten*, The Slow Loris Press, *Some*, *Southern Poetry*, *Sou'wester*, *Street*, *Sumac*, *Survivor's Manual*, *Tennessee Poetry Journal*, *Unmuzzled Ox*.

The author wishes to thank the John Simon Guggenheim Memorial Foundation for the leisure time during which many of these poems were written.

Contents

Facing the Tree

INVOCATION

Dirt and stone, if I may know you as you know
    yourselves,
if you do have sense of yourselves,
I walk upon and study you as my next brothers and
    sisters,
in this only way I know how to think about you.
I pick you up in my hands and run you slowly through
    my fingers,
I feel so close to you, if only not to fear
but to know and make you my kin, even if I must do
    it alone.
I am resigned, if I must say it that way.
Try as I might, I cannot think myself exactly that.
I see us each in separate worlds
and because I must join yours and gradually become
    as you,
I want to know what home will be like there.

If I could say that from you can be made men and
    women,
how happy and relieved I'd be to know
we have a sort of exchange program between us,
in which we spring up out of the dust
and are greeted with open arms to tell that all is well
back there growing its fruits.
And then to embrace, all of us together,

and celebrate with drink and dancing
and to see one into the soil
with solemn benedictions on a current of joy,
waving him farewell as he disintegrates to dust.

I speak to you in pity for myself; speak to me
and return the love I must have for you,
since I must be buried one day in you
and would go towards love again, as in life.
Let us be reconciled to one another.
Dirt and stone into which my flesh will turn,
this much we have in common. As I cannot speak to
    my bones
nor my blood nor my own flesh, why then must I
    speak?
What says I must speak if I am not answered?
What then that I should speak or am I speaking at all,
if my own flesh and bones cannot answer me,
as if already they were partners of the stones and dirt?

Part I

READING THE HEADLINES

I have a burial ground in me where I place the bodies
without fuss or emotion, hundreds of thousands at a
  glance.
I stow them in and as it happens I am eating dinner,
I continue to eat, feeding myself and the dead.

I walk around in this burial ground, examining it
with curiosity, find it dark but stroll with a sense
of safety, my own place. I want to lie down in it,
dissatisfied with it, true, but seeing no exit, I lie
down to rest and dream.

I am lost anyway, without horizon or recognizable
  features.
It's just to walk on. At least it's not necessary
to kill myself. I'll die of attrition of my energy to live.

I know my direction and have companions, after all.

I'M HERE

The radio said, Go to your shelters,
in such a low whisper that we stood there
in front of the set, not wanting to understand
it was not part of a play. The color
of the blast came high over the horizon.
We stood watching it, still unable to realize
that we were being killed, for real.

We ran and are still running, it seems,
though our bodies have long since dropped
from us. We could be the wind rushing
through the trees or the stars moving out
to the perimeter. We know we felt ourselves
vanishing in flame and wind
and it seemed as though we were becoming
one or the other.

How then can we still speak to you
without body or voice? Do you know
there is another world, very silent,
which penetrates this one you're in?
Without your knowledge or your feeling it
you hear every word I speak but do not see
or feel me anywhere at all. I have no sight
or touch of you but I speak because I am

from nowhere in particular. And now
can you tell me what it is to live?

Are you lying in a cave at rest?
Or waiting crouched for the enemy,
or do you have your family with you still,
comforting them with food?
What is your situation?
Once having been human like you, if I may presume
nothing for you has changed in form, body
or mind, I hunger for a voice to fill
an emptiness in my speech,
which perhaps is what makes me invisible.
You can speak to me by standing perfectly still
where you are and breathing regularly.
Then I'll understand that all is well
for the human and leave,
content.

LETTER TO A FRIEND

Yesterday I killed a man. It was such a surprise to me. I was driving along in my car, taking it easy, stopping at red lights and starting up leisurely, knowing the next light was timed to turn red before I could reach it.

I was not racing, I was not impatient. I was not trying to do the unusual or unexpected, when as if from beneath the pavement he sprang up in front of my car. Was it from beneath? I'm too dazed to know and almost delighted at being completely innocent in the law.

They say that where I ran him down the tar is ripped open as if he might have torn through from beneath, but he's dead and no one can explain.

There's no sewer below from which to spring; just plain dirt that once was farm land, not so long ago. I was here when the pavement was laid down. Could it have been the farmer who sold the land, protesting after taking the money, his conscience bothering him? Or a fertility god? I don't believe in such things.

Could I have been dreaming at the wheel? Had this man been lying in the road already hurt, unable to rise quickly and I caught up in thought, the ride going smoothly?

But why should I question myself? I did right, I stopped the car, I got out and ran back to pick him up, and as I raised his head it began to come apart in my hand like the broken head of a doll. I put it right back on the ground, I called the police, they questioned me for hours, I answered patiently, convinced of my innocence, and I was released.

They smiled at each other, as if they knew something they would not tell me. At least I'm innocent and I have killed a man. What a curious sensation. I wonder will it ever happen again.

MY PRESIDENT WEEPS

The President's blood is on my hands; he has taken another decision, this time to smash the dikes. His life is full of weeping in self-pity at the cruelties he must impose, and blood pours from his eyes at the intensity of grief. Standing beside him, with my hands reaching to comfort him, they are covered with his blood, but he pushes me off and is harsh, telling me to leave or be killed too. I leave.

He does not know I already am dead. He has taken the position that all must die and he has taken the position knowingly and has built it out of thoughts about freedom and independence and the rights of man. Such a President who lingers in the gardens of the future to be able to pluck one flower that he could bring to life.

Blood covers him entirely from his weeping eyes. My President, my poems that are stained with blood, poems in which the blood runs down the page, poems that have holes in them the size of shrapnel wounds, poems that peel off from paper like napalmed skin, poems that crumple together like the gassed, poems that eat themselves in agony like village animals, their guts hanging out in the rice fields after bombing. My President weeps and weeps and I tear my arms from their sockets, my fingers from their joints, my hair from its roots, my eyes from their sockets to tell you my President weeps and looks darkly back at us from the television.

I WONDER WHO IS NEXT

Listen, Mao Tsetung will live forever; they are giving him a lung transplant, he smokes too much, and a heart transplant, and all his other organs are under acupuncture. They keep an eye on his pulse and watch his every fragile move. When he speaks they record his voice for significant variations and his handwriting is scrutinized. Wherever he walks or sits they surround him in a crowd from head to foot. He becomes invisible. Live forever, Mao Tsetung.

MY ENEMIES

I know how I have learned to hate. I've turned on trees and animals and crushed the ant in my path. Many a time I've ignored the sun and the moon in my walk to keep my eyes turned down toward the dirt of the path or its concrete and often refused to wash my body of its sweat and oils. I saw no purpose in a tree growing or in the food set before me. I could see no commerce between men and me. Did the stars touch each other? Did they reach out to give light when the light failed in another? Was the sun sympathetic? Did the moon care? Did my feet warn me of the creatures beneath their soles as I walked? Who held me in such regard as to want to unburden me of my faults and let me live? It was a concert of divisiveness without any particular foe or intention: a salad of kinds of separateness on which I was fed, and because I lived I wondered about all this and remarked on my living. Why, I asked myself, was it not possible to name the faults and hold them as a keepsake for the living? I did this and I survived my pain and everything about the sun was granted for what it was and everything about my parents and my brothers, my food and the soles of my shoes and the separateness of stars and the purpose lacking in the trees and my own divisiveness. Granting all this and knowing that

I had brought my own death closer by living this day
I thought of such a thing as love to describe it.

I greet the hair on my head and chest and pubic re-
gion each morning as my companions in living. I ex-
pose my teeth to welcome them in my mouth, teeth
that stay with me out of loyalty or their own desire
to remain and be. I am prepared now for loving the
day. I can be hurt and I brood.

I may take my quiet revenge but hurt and brooding
and revenge absorb me even deeper in this meaning,
that my life loves my toenails even as I love my ene-
mies.

I SHOWED HIM MY WOUND

I showed him my wound and he said it was not there. Then where is it, I asked, touching it. Ask yourself, he replied; and as I rose up into the air, following his flight, how did I manage to levitate, I asked myself somewhat fearfully. I was elated, my wound was not hurting and he had disappeared. Who is he, I wondered. Who am I speaking about? Where did I get the notion about an other? Did I hear a voice? Did someone speak to me? But in the air, trying to make out that other who already had disappeared, I begin to speak with two voices, one addressing me and the other answering. The wound was throbbing; it was located between my legs. It yearned for a scar to heal it. There was nothing I could do but wish in a third voice, a tremolo. I was speaking with three voices, and I felt myself in the company of strangers. Ha, I said to myself, I am having a conversation with that other who did, after all, speak to me originally. I was not dreaming, but I dreamed on and I was always happy.

You can find me in my bed, bleeding but strong. I am afloat in my blood. It has become my bed. I lie back upon a pillow of coagulated blood and from there I observe the steady trickling of my wound, but I am so peaceful and contented. The pain has stopped; the ache has disappeared, and I have been flying in bed. I feel I am inhabited by another being, and that's what makes me so happy scared, scared to lose consciousness of myself, for I am so glad to suffer. At least, to suffer is to know I am and yet I am happy, flying in bed, bleeding but strong, about to lose myself in terror, three voices: mine questioning and being answered, with the third observing and noting and urging me to die for the sake of happiness. I am in the middle of the earth.

I knew I could persuade myself to die in an ecstatic voice, and I will live in every element, but now let me think about it as faithfully as I can to make it mine, and let me think in this third voice until this body is its dream.

The fork I raise to my mouth should be the fork in a dream; the kiss I give should be the kiss given in a dream. The dream I would be having would be of the world being dreamed as it should be: of sequences, the creator at the center — me who could dream the world or not but with preference for the dream flowing, enchanting in the ease it could be lived or turned off: the feel of a fork in my hand like that of silk. In the world where the steel for it is made the fork is hard and pointed. How may I live in silkiness until the dream brings me to a death entered with a silky ease.

THE DINER

If I order a sandwich and get a plate of ham and eggs instead, has communication broken down? Is there a chef in the house? There's no chef. I get only silence. Who brought me the ham and eggs? I was sitting at the counter when it arrived. I don't remember anyone bringing it. I'm leaving right now to find another place to eat in, a bit more congenial than this silence, with no one to witness that I ordered exactly what I say I did. But now the door is closed and I can't leave.

Will someone please open the door, the one who gave me the ham and eggs instead of a sandwich? If I'm dissatisfied and want to leave why must I stay? Can the proprietor do as he pleases with anyone on his property? Am I his property too? What do you know! I have to eat what's given me or go hungry. I have to be nice about it too and say thank you to the silence. But I want to know why I can't have what I want that's such an innocent wish as between a sandwich and a plate of ham and eggs? What have I said or did I say what I thought I did or am I in my own country where my language is spoken? Where am I? Why can't I leave this diner? This is not my country. I don't belong here. I never even got a passport to come. I don't remember leaving. I don't remember crossing the border and I'm the only guy here at the counter. Something phony is going on. Somebody is trying to drive me nuts or rob me or kill me. I want to go back where I came from. I was on the road hungry, driving. It was dark and I hadn't eaten my dinner.

You know, it's quite possible I made these ham and eggs myself instead of a sandwich. It may be I'm the owner because no one else is here and I have the key to open the door, exactly like my car key. I must have arranged it that way. Now when in hell did I buy this diner and who needs it!

THE ASSASSIN

Stare into the gun barrel, a wildly grinning man behind it, and think twice; first to save yourself, next to reconcile yourself to dying. Plead for your life and offer treasures of your soul: your human love, recognition of his life, your wish to know him as a person. He slowly squeezes at the trigger, satisfied that what he's heard is nonsense to a man who knows this is the way to prove himself a human like the others. His eyes widen, lips slowly open to speak or to swallow. A noise, you're hit: your life inside intensifies, you cannot stop yourself from falling at his feet. Your head is drained of strength, a peace is filling it. You lift your face to let him see what he too can expect one day as a blessing, and your eyes close on his amazed expression.

TALKING TO MYSELF

About my being a poet, the trees certainly haven't expressed an interest, standing at a distance. I'd expect that at least they'd try to learn something new besides growing their leaves, old stuff by now, and anyway it's done by so many others. Wouldn't these trees want to know what they'll be doing in a hundred years, what they look like now, how they stand, what's their name, where they are and what they actually do in winter and in summer, deaf, dumb and happy as they are? Not happy, simply willing to go on like always. Not even willing, just doing what comes naturally. To them I might as well be dead or a tree.

To stay among the trees as if I were at home, arrived from a long journey, I am digging a place for a burial with my feet.

NOW CELEBRATE LIFE AND DEATH

CROATIAN GUERRILLAS
EXECUTED IN YUGOSLAVIA
— News Report

The Croatians watching the soldiers line up in front of them for the execution and then feeling the bullets enter their heads and chests, does this have anything in common with the man who inserts his penis into the vagina where he also feels himself while the woman feels herself? Did the Croatians live for the shots to enter and the man for his penis to enter in order for the woman to feel herself a body, therefore a being, a person she would want herself to be called then, very pleased and flattered that she has made the man feel himself in her as the man is pleased that he can make her feel herself through him: giving each other to confirm bodily existence. And so how should the Croatians feel toward their executioners and the executioners toward their victims? Can each take pride in the others' bodily feelings arising from actions each must perform? May they give thanks to each other, the executioners for feeling their power to kill and exercising it with efficiency and terror and finally guilty but thankful, for without feeling they do not exist, and the executed, as they sink to their knees bullet-laden, may thank the firing squad for having given them to feel their identity this intensely at its

last moments. So eat and fill your mouth and discover
the response in yourself, you becoming aware of taste
buds that please your palate that make your body you.
Now celebrate life and death for this reason.

INFORMATION

This tree has two million and seventy-five thousand
   leaves.
Perhaps I missed a leaf or two but I do feel triumphant
at having persisted in counting by hand branch by
   branch
and marked down on paper with pencil each total.
Adding them up was a pleasure I could understand.
I did something on my own that was not dependent
   on others,
and to count leaves is not less meaningful than to
   count
the stars, as astronomers are always doing. They want
the facts to be sure they have them all. It would help
them to know whether the world is finite. I discovered
one tree that is finite. I must try counting the hairs
on my head, and you too. We could swap informa-
tion.

Make up a poem about a man going to sleep in his business clothes to wake up in a hospital in a pair of regulation hospital pajamas. He demands to be let out but they tell him he fell asleep on the job and so must have something wrong with him. He insists nothing is wrong. He was tired and that was all. How can it be tiredness only, they insist, when he let the phone ring all day and night while sleeping in his chair at the desk. It was only when his wife came looking for him in panic that he was discovered. "Did I let the phone ring all day and night?" "Yes," they reply gently to mark their concern for him and to let him know he's under their care. "Well, perhaps I wanted to," he replies vigorously, and starts to climb out of bed. They forcefully restrain him and he begins to shout. "But we have taken a cardiogram of your heart while you were asleep and it exhibited a dangerous slowness." "I was hibernating," he shouts. "We took a reading of your brain waves and they were virtually still." "I was hibernating. I was a bear and now I am a man again!" Oh, then he is insane, they tell each other with their eyes and insanity is the cause. We can't let him go back to his business. "You are not feeling well," they tell him softly, holding him tightly to the bed. "Of course I am insane!" he shouts. "So what of it! I want to be insane. I'm entitled to be insane, if I want to be! I'll even shit in this bed to prove it to you. Nothing can stop me and if you don't release me

I'll have to harm myself to prove to you that freeing me is the better policy." His logic is distorted, they decide and find no choice within themselves but to keep him under restraint. Then you don't want to go back to your business, they probe to prove to him that he is not fit to lead a normal life. "But I do want to go back to my business! I do want to run it as I've always done and I've always been insane! My business permits me to be insane, in fact encourages me and supports me and nourishes my insanity, so what the hell, you're holding back a good man." And they were baffled. What kind of disease is this? They had to think, but first they had to tie him down with straps to secure him to the bed after which they left to consult among themselves in private, and they think they have had a very queer experience themselves, listening to his logic and conviction. They have to laugh. Out of insanity, he had said, he had founded his business, made it profitable for himself. Was it a way to live, they wondered, and the question remained unanswered because their own lives already seemed peculiar to them but enjoyable, having to deal with this kind of patient who made them sense their own peculiar condition, to have to dwell on him. Were they insane in their way and was it dangerous while enjoyable or was it dangerous because it was enjoyable? They put themselves in complete dilemma about it but accepted it as a dilemma which spurred them on, fed on the occupation they had chosen which they could concede had its own logic. Their faces betrayed no horror. They meant to keep on and would resist any attempt within themselves or from the patient to condemn their practice and seek his release.

A TRIPTYCH

Holding off the mugger who never knew you, never met you, never suffered through your deeds, everything is fine, you keep screaming as you kick him in the groin and then swing your foot straight up into his belly to lay him out unconscious, and he dies — internal hemorrhage. Cops open notebooks in their hands, their faces bent upon the page, suspicious, apathetic, indifferent and displeased to have to think of you, a stranger. You have a kind of stranglehold upon their thought, you've blocked their easy breathing in the night. They take you in, they want to know what were you doing on the street the very moment that the mugger showed himself. Open your life, how when you spoke last to your wife it was to tell her the world extended in so many directions from the house. That does it and you're booked. One turns and grabs you by the throat and you stand together at the sergeant's desk to round out a world.

II

"Out of evil cometh good." Let me think now: the strangler will have picked my pockets, about ten dollars. He will have had the satisfaction of getting away with it again and be able to buy himself a new fix. My

wife will collect on my insurance and clear the mort-
gage on the house. I think she will cry for days, as
will my daughter. I don't know about my son, he
may think about the dangers of walking the streets at
night. Do I want to die to hasten these events?

I know the city will survive my death, and when I
consider that policemen are needed at their posts and
mailmen must continue to deliver their mail or wel-
fare checks and prize announcements, and funerals
must be held and bodies buried to keep the smell and
infestation from the living, all's well about my dying.
I wonder then that I hesitate to submit to his hands. I
too must carry on as usual which is my peace, the
trains on time, the meal served when needed, the
water on tap and grass, trees and birds as I require
them, everything in its place: death, love, happiness,
warmth and job security. I'm all for them. Kill me
when you must, mugger.

III

I should believe that a man being mugged in his own
apartment is part of the order of things. I'm sad about
this, one of the last among the non-mugged, an old
order vanishing into hospitals. Should I turn mugger
too, writing about it in secret between jobs? I see a
still younger generation on the horizon standing in

armies waiting to advance. We of the earlier order of muggers would then have to salute as they attack us and pray they prosper in their trade and learn to be outraged when mugged in turn to feel themselves estranged in their own land or escaped north among the Eskimos who wear thick gloves and cannot mug efficiently.

CODA

A man sitting on the ground with his head in his hands, he no longer understands himself. His body forms an enclosure; his head in his hands is his world, he holds his world in his hands and it feels the pressure of his fingers in despair. When he dies it will be as if he has gone to live, and so he lies back upon the ground, his one other abiding contact, and is at peace, having given himself.

I could spend my life contemplating the weaving back and forth of the topmost branches with no visible force moving them. I could imagine they do this of their own free will. I know a log is lying across two stones to make a bench but to sit upon it is to confirm this knowledge. I know that a bullet shot out of a gun can pierce the heart but to confirm it I would have to pull the trigger aimed at you, only for the sake of knowledge. I know nothing beyond this method to help me know.

Part II

IN A DREAM

at fifty I approach myself,
eighteen years of age,
seated despondently on the concrete steps
of my father's house,
wishing to be gone from there
into my own life,
and I tell my young self,
Nothing will turn out right,
you'll want to revenge yourself,
on those close to you especially,
and they will want to die,
of shock and grief. You will fall
to pleading and tears of self-pity,
filled with yourself, a passionate stranger.
My eighteen-year-old self stands up
from the concrete steps and says,
Go to hell,
and I walk off.

THINKING

I am caught in the body of a fish.
If I am the fish itself this speech
is the sound of water escaping
through my gills and like all fish
I will be caught in the mouth
of a larger one or be netted
or die of being fish. Thinking
that I am caught inside, a person
with a right to freedom as I've been
trained to think, my thought is another
kind of net because this right
to freedom is a torment like being
caught in the body of a fish.

BIOGRAPHY

In these typewriter keys is the story of my parents
   and me
that I will not give the keys to type,
the three of us held in tension
I do not want interrupted,
unable to resolve the differences between us
and they are dead.

THE WEATHER

Live for myself
said the wind
Live for myself
said the rain
Live for myself
said the night
I bent my head
turned up my collar

My poetry is for the night
of empty buses. I write,
depleted and hug my death.
Live for others, I hear whispered,
for the child growing,
face of a rushing stream.

I fall asleep
as it were a poem
being written
to resolve my cares
into a final solution
and as my eyes close
and silence spreads itself
inside me like a wave
I know I am succeeding,
and in sleep rejoice.

There must be something wrong with me
wanting to keep going through
the endless griefs as if I had iron
bowels and a stone head
and perhaps it is stone and iron
in me now thinking.

MY OWN LINE

I try to follow through the maze
by holding on with both hands
and slowly threading, picking out the knots
and tangles. Sometimes when I disentangle them
I stand confused, looking around for what is mine
and can't find it and am lost and panicky,
so many look alike, so many more tempting
in color and strength and others taut
and keen. I am afraid of them, incapable
of handling any, adapted only to my own
these many years, and when I find it
at the bottom of the heap
or somewhere in the middle, gray colored,
obscured almost, I grab it in relief,
freed of my uncertainty and hang on
grimly and move ahead through the whirring
jungle of lines above, beneath and around me,
gnashing my teeth in hope
to find my way out into the clear
to where my line is leading,
slack at both ends.

THE REFUSE MAN

I'm going to pull my stinking wagon
through the streets and countryside,
letting it smell up the highways
and its odor crawl into the one-
and two-family houses along the road
and over the corn and wheatfields
and let the cows raise their heads
from munching to bellow their anger
and the cop to draw up alongside
my wagon — I'll be pulling it
between the shafts — and let this cop,
holding his nose, come over to ask
in an awed voice what the hell
it is I'm hauling and I'll tell him,
as sweetly as I can, "A dish of rotted guts,
an empty skull, a fetid breast, a swarming
belly, a corpse, a man right out
of his mother's belly given his occupation,
and I've put myself between the shafts —
a horse will not come near this;
I had to, being a man."

IN THIS DREAM

a vacuum cleaner held over my head
is drawing out my brains through my nostrils,
blood running in a column straight up
into the vacuum bag whining like a jet engine.
I feel my intestines too beginning to move up
through my gullet and soon they will be pouring
through my nose. My bones quiver in their sockets,
my knees are shaking. I sit down,
emptiness is becoming me. I can no longer think,
I just listen to the sucking vacuum.
Here goes my heart, straight up into my throat
and choking me, pumping in my throat.
It is filling my mouth, it is forcing its way
between my teeth. The vacuum roars
and my mouth flies open and my heart is gone.

How is it I keep writing?
The vacuum roars and whines alternately,
my ears stick to my head but now my head
is rising, a wind is whistling through my skull.
My head is being lifted from my neck.
Take me altogether, great vacuum:
my arms, legs, sex, shoes, clothes,
my pen gripped in my whitened hand
drained of blood. Take me altogether
and I triumph, whirled in the vacuum bag
with my satellite heart, brain, bones and blood.

Said a voice to me
from the pillow
Ho Ho I am Bill Williams
Write me a poem
about yourself
Are you afraid?
Get it down
say it say it say it

I lifted my head
dazed
my stomach turning
gray dawn at the window
my senses flowing back on me
swinging me over and over
over and under an ocean
isolating me
from wife and child

BACKYARD

When I wake up in the morning I'm scattered
over a gray landscape, my arms and legs
immobilized. I don't see the connection
between myself and a finch warbling
in the rising sun. I want
an explanation of the world.

Catbird complaining in the sun
for something nobody knows what.
He flies away, can't make himself understood
like other birds. He'll settle for bugs
as they come out of hiding
after rain.

SPINNING

I have my hands out to you
but you say your hands
do not exist. You also say
that I do not have hands,
that I have an illusion of hands
and that speaking to you
is speaking to myself,
appealing to myself
to be at one with me.
You show me what you mean
by spinning, standing
in one place — a humming top.
It delights you
and you urge me on.
I begin to turn
as I begin to weep.

Where is a rock to bore a hole through?
I need to find a rock to drill
a look through to the other side.
Any rock, any ordinary species.
I'll be happy with a rock.

WITH MY BACK

With my back to the insane world
of the next room I look into my poetry
for the gentleness in making do
with the known facts. On his side
of the wall sits a young man
spilling fear from his mouth.
I read in my poetry that fear teaches
me to love and that love also
is the beginning of fear
so that I find myself upon a cutting edge.
He in the room next door is bloody,
I look in my poetry for what to do
to help and read I must remain
absolutely still. He must be allowed
to think he is alone and that the world
waits on him for decision.

THE FUTURE

I am going to leave a child in an empty room.
She will have my body to look down on
at my death, when she will ask of the room
its address, the room silent,
stretching across the sky.
What comfort for her, my only expectation,
as in her infancy she climbs upon my lap?

My daughter, as I recede into the past,
I give you this
worth more than money,
more than a tip on the market:
keep strong;
prepare to live without me
as I am prepared.

BIRDS IN WINTER

At the command
they rise trembling on air
and fly off in formation.
Offspring will return
who cannot be told
from their parents.

Peace belongs with the birds,
buffeted by wind,
driven close to the wave's lash.
They have found a place
for storms in their brain;
utter no protest,
their wings widespread.

Somehow it does not write itself, our life together,
my need expressed by your giving,
my seeking satisfied with your finding.
Truly we fit like bolt in lock,
to keep our house free of childishness and pretension;
love not in rhetoric,
emotion not in eyes.
When I feel your leg thrown over me in sleep
I say, That is the thought.

Part III

He moves straight before him, legs moving lightly
over ground. Encounters a lamppost
with caressing hands, moves on
to meet a water hydrant he lightly vaults,
eyes lifted to the tall buildings
irregular in height. Smiling as if amused
in sleep he climbs rapidly up one wall.
Tenants sip their coffee and look down
into the street or from the window talk
to someone in the room. He nears the very top
of one skyscraper, lifts a window and steps in
and strides to the other end of the room
and through its wall. Around him conversation
never stops, an office of whirring typewriters.
In the corridor, emerging from the wall,
as he turns to an exit marked by a red light
he meets her on the stairs.

                              They come together,
fuse, her breast becomes his left chest,
his lower lip rouged, right arm muscular,
the left soft, round and exposed at the shoulder,
right hip shaped like a female's
and on his left foot a black high-heeled pump,
his right leg covered by a half skirt.

Still he is smiling but even more broadly
as in sleep. In the hallway where he stands
transformed people rush by to and from
elevators opening and closing.

He explodes.

EACH DAY

Cynthia Matz, with my finger in your cunt
and you sliding back and forth on it,
protesting at the late hour and tiredness
and me with kidneys straining to capacity
with piss I had no chance to release
all night, we got up from the park bench
and walked you home. I left you
at the door, you said something
dispiriting about taking a chance
and settling on me. I had left Janette
to chase after you running out
of the ice cream parlor where the three
of us had sat — I had felt so sorry
and so guilty to have you find me
with her in the street. You and I
had gone to shows together,
you needed me to talk to and I was glad.
The talk always was about him
whom you still loved and he had jilted
you for someone else. I'm sorry, Cynthia,
that it had to end this way between us too,
I did not return the next day,
after leaving you at the door.
I did not return the following day either.
I went with Janette in whom I felt
nothing standing in the way,

while with you it would have been
each day to listen to your sadness
at having been betrayed by him.
I was not to be trusted either,
I too wanted love pure and simple.

FINGERNAILS

They look long enough to bite and I attack them with my
teeth, feeling the satisfaction of cutting short an
aggression. I am biting into myself, cutting myself down,
swallowing what I have bitten off to assure its growing back.

I need to cut it down over and over. I am paying for
something wrong but assuring myself of the satisfaction
of seeing that wrong grow back so that I'll have the pleasure
of cutting it down again: sex love: physical love. I fill
my mouth with bitten, sharp fingernails. I could swallow
my whole hand.

In the silence we sat across the table
from each other — always there was some obstacle
between us — and bit into our food.
It was our love for one another
disappearing down our throats
never again to emerge
except as waste.

A MORAL TALE

All this for me, he asked,
looking down on her body.
Uh huh, she said, arms stretched out
upon the bed, and she looked up at him
with an amused smile. I think
I'll take it, he said,
and wrapped it up in the sheet
that lay beneath her. He brought
the four ends together in a knot
and slung the body across his back.
He was on his way home to show
his latest find. He had discovered
each body was different
and that altogether they amounted
to a survey of the female form,
something an anthropologist could appreciate,
and he was thinking of becoming one
but there was a hitch; he was bringing
back more bodies than with place
to store them in the house
and it was expensive elsewhere,
at a cost. He persisted.
He went broke;
his wife left him.
He had to give up his studies;
he had to go back to work

and was left with memories
which to relieve himself in his unhappiness
he would relate at work
where in amazement he was urged to write them
down.
The manuscript was published.
The book sold.
There was money again
to return to his studies.

Moral: In adversity we find our goal in life.

I give you a little stick, you give me a tiny pebble. We're exciting each other to think differently of ourselves, and we can see an opening in each other that will lead to music and to dance. I probe with the stick, you press with the pebble against my flesh. It hurts, but it's meaningful and we're in love.

Once there was a woman smiled at me
from her open door. I wanted her
at once and sat through a political
meeting in her house, thinking
of just this.

AT THIS MOMENT

I'm very pleased to be a body. Can there be someone without a body? As you hold mine I feel firmly assured that bodies are the right thing and I think all life is a body. I'm happy about trees, grass and water, especially with the sun shining on it. I slip into it, a summer pleasure.

I have hurt the body. That's when I know I need it most in its whole condition. If I could prove it to you by giving pain you would agree but I prefer you with your body pressed to mine as if to say it is how we know. Think, when two must separate how sad it is for each then having to find another way to affirm their bodies. Knock one against another or tree or rock and there's your pain. Now we have our arms filled with each other. Could we not grow old in this posture and be buried as one body which others would do for us tenderly?

ZOO

Behind bars
a tiger
moving like striped silk —
a work of art
I want to worship
at its paws.

Part IV

AUTUMN I

The trees are standing like silent members
of a crowd awaiting decision. They are
rigid and erect, the verdict a foregone
conclusion. I stand before them
guilty but wanting to live —
unsure of myself, timid,
my shoulders hunched.

                                 I straighten up
and sing. They remain silent.
I turn around and march off,
working my arms up and down
like a soldier. Having nowhere to go,
nothing in particular to do,
I keep marching.

AUTUMN

(For Wendell Berry)

A leaf lies shaking
at my door, about to be
blown away.
           If I should
bring it into the still
air of my room, it would
lie quietly on the windowsill
facing the tree
from which it fell.

FOR . . .

Poet of dead farms
dried-up riverbeds and burnt grass
has taken himself to a white room
with barred window to think himself
alive, breathing in, beating his chest
in joy and shout good tidings
to the trees of his outlook.
What of insanity? For love delivers
him to his foes, praising their hatred
and his guilt. His head hurts,
he is sick to his stomach for coming back
to life in a barred room
the key in his head, love the key:
a dead farm and parched scrub grass.
Abandonment is what he knows.

FOR JOHN BERRYMAN

You're dead, what can I do for you?
I am not unsympathetic;
I thought about you often enough
though we never spoke together
but once when I shied away,
feeling something that I fought
in me too — and came out with this
manner of living, by living.

It is depressing to live
but to kill myself in protest
is to assume there is something
to life withheld from me, yet
who withholds it? Think about it.
What is the answer?

But suicide is not so wrong
for one who thought and prayed
his way toward it. I wish, though,
I had known sooner, to have
helped you go on living,
as I do, half a suicide,
the need defended by the other half
that thinks to live in that knowledge
is praiseworthy.

EXPRESS YOUR WILL

Seeing a patch of sky through the trees
I look for a paratrooper
to float down through the leaves
and to beg pardon for his intrusion
and to ask if I enjoy the weather,
sunny and mild. Of course, of course,
I'll answer enthusiastically and he
will unlimber his gun from his shoulder
and fill me with lead.

I thought so, he will say.
I expected you would find the weather good.
Now take a look at me, he will add,
and turn the gun on himself
and pull the trigger. That's to show you
what I really think, he'll say.
But I'll be dead, leaving him for others
to study.

Change, change, change
into a paratrooper.
Make yourself a hunter,
kill,
express your will.

SH, THIS POEM WANTS TO SAY
SOMETHING

Yes, I was out to visit with my friends
at the bar yesterday when one spoke up
about having a problem. I asked casually
what it could be, with him standing here,
glass in hand, drinking beside me,
and he said, "The problem is me.
I'm wondering what to do with myself
every day, now that there's nothing
to live for except myself."
And I blinked and thought about that
for a while and replied, That is a problem.
Why not live for me or for your other friends?
How else could we get to meet,
with you gone and then maybe John and Jack
and Jane, each of us taking your position
and doing away with ourselves? My friend
looked at me for a moment briefly
and asked, "Is that so?"
and we exchanged glances, smiled
and emptied our glasses.

In this dream I'm an Indian
confronted by a military commander,
his regiment behind him, seeking
to intimidate me into going away.
I am pointing to earth and sky
to say I am of both
and that it is they who leave
when I go.

       At this, I must wake up
to warn that if what he says is true
all of us are lost. I am the commander's
countryman and in my dream I urge
him to take off his uniform
at once and go bathing
in the nearest spring.

In the end is the word to destroy the world
and make a word of it alone
sitting over the water like a cloud
an atomic whitish cloud
like the frost of one's winter breath
To draw one's breath is to destroy
the world and make a fine haze of it.

FOR MARIANNE MOORE

In her garden were flowers
she had not yet named
but they had sprung up
at her consent
and she waited
for the moment
they would become
their colors and their shape
of leaves, for though she saw
them it was not for her
to name them
and to lose their life
in words.

I shake my fist at a tree
and say, You will shed your leaves
in time for all your abundance
and variety but I will see to it
that you continue in your present
state in my mind. You have no
memory except in me. I'm
about to write of you
leaf by leaf.

Those dead brown leaves lying at my door
as if to let me see them in their last condition
before they disappear into the fields, I am
your only witness. If I live to have
to see you dead, then there is no answer
to your death but life, and I am living it.

THE LEGEND OF YOUTH

In the small square to which we had confined our-
    selves,
all openings exposed, our fear at a minimum,
finally forgotten, it struck. One of us
rolled upon the ground, the ball locked in his arms.
In the game's excitement he may have tripped;
we could not tell. He did not rise.
There was no sign, nothing had reached out.
We laid him aside and went on,
our glances furtive upon him as we played —
when the next, the ball clasped to his chest,
upright, eyes wide, pitched forward upon his face.
We knew then, and now among the many
in this small square where they lie
in the postures they were caught in,
my back bent far over as a shield,
I sneak a glance
at where the sun stood
and see shadow.

SUBWAY

I thought that if he could stoop
to pick out rubbish, each piece
placed in his bag — a tedious job
in front of crowds, all day
the trains at a steady roar,
the lighting dim, the air stagnant —
from bin to bin, searching
to the bottom for gum wrappers,
crumpled newspapers, torn sandwich
bags, cigarette stubs, particles
clinging to his fingers. All this
without a word, bending
at the foot of a steel pillar,
it was not too much for me
to be witness.

THE PLEASURE

I enjoy watching myself
grow old and gray
I am authentic I say
I belong with the others.

When news came of his death I was disappointed.
How many times have I turned away
from silence in a room or among people
and begun to talk into the phone
or nudged a neighbor in a crowd?
I wasn't given brain, tongue, ears, hands,
feet to dwell on silence. I'm sorry
he's dead, and it surely is a disappointment
to him too where he lies, unable to speak
or to move or to make a sign,
so then let us do for him
what he would do for himself, if he could:
ignore this death.

GOING DOWN

There's a hole in the earth I'm afraid of.
I lower myself into it, first tying
one end of a long rope to a tree close by,
the other end around my waist.
I let myself down hand over hand,
gripping the rope hard,
with each step planting my feet
solidly against the sides
that give off an earth odor.

As I descend I breathe less of air
and more a mingling of minerals and clay,
wet, heavy, close. I begin to lose
consciousness and I am afraid
I will loosen my grip on the rope
and fall to the bottom and be suffocated
by dirt chunks falling on top of me
from off the walls. It was this
fear of burial led me to climb down.

IN SEASON

I have enemies among the leaves.
Listen to the whispering
and the rubbing of bodies
to get close together on the plot.
I'll turn my back
and let them go on with their heated talk
as I await their downfall
in season.

LINGUISTICS

I heard a man without a tongue talking.
He grunted grammatically.
It was easy to grasp that he wanted a tongue
and was saying he missed it.
I was quite moved and I was delighted
he could signal
but who could help?
What could be done
except to teach him to write
and make that his subject.
We'd embrace him,
knowing that among us were legs,
arms, heads and penises missing
that we could talk about endlessly,
alone.

MELPOMENE IN MANHATTAN

As she walked she would look back
over her shoulder and trip
upon sidewalk cracks or bump
into people to whom she would apologize
profusely, her head still turned.
One could hear her murmur to herself
tearfully, as though filled with a yearning
to recover what she was leaving behind
as if she would preserve it
or do for it what she had neglected
out of ignorance or oversight
or from sheer meanness and spite
or simple helplessness to do better,
her voice beginning to keen
as she tripped or steered blindly
into the gutter
or into hostile crowds.

THEIR MOUTHS FULL

Let there be ripeness, said the Lord.
And men bowed down to see brown in the pod
and to its meat palpable and sweet.
And of this fruit you shall eat
for your wisdom, said the Lord.
And of none other, lest you die.
And the men ate of the ripened fruit
and rejoiced in its taste
and of the seed split between their teeth,
for these too were sweet of their kind;
and so it happened that unripened fruit
was looked on with scorn
and beaten down from its branches
in the Lord's name as sinful
and the work of death.
And men sat themselves down to grow
palpable and sweet to one another
in the sun and it was then time to die,
ripening, and they died,
blessing their maker,
their mouths full of one another.

PROSE POEM IN SIX PARTS

I'm so happy, he shouts, as he puts a bullet through his head. It leaves a clean hole on either side of the skull, no blood pouring out. I'm so happy, he shouts at his triumph. He knew it would happen this way, pulling the trigger. He knew it, he had imagined it and he collapses of a spasm of joy.

His friends look closely at the clean hole on either side and decide to take their own thoughts seriously too and act. It will not be with a pistol but with each other whom they have had on their minds for so long without daring to speak openly about it. They speak and become transfixed in each other's image. They are not exactly dead, they are unmoving but fulfilled. They are not even aware of being happy or depressed and the domestic animals that roam among them nibbling at their fingers, ears, toes and nose is how these animals eat at flowers and grass. To the transfixed it is a happy identification. They can believe the world is whole, all this without saying a word, their eyes starry.

II

Their eyes starry, their bodies glistening with sweat that acts like a lacquer to seal their pores, they grow rigid, gleam like polished stone. They can recall the one who put a bullet through his head. He has risen and walks among them tapping on each body for a response to his happiness, each tap like his heartbeat to inform each rigid body exhibiting its own happiness. These are mutually dependent acts but tapping his way from body to body, his imagination proven to him, he is not aware of their happiness while the one person who is aware of this dilemma has not yet shot himself in the head or talked to another human about each other. He could be lonely were it not for the sight of these who are so happy in themselves. They promise much and he has a relative hope for the future.

III

He has a relative hope for the future. He lights up a cigar and observes the community of polished stones and the one pierced skull and wishes to make himself totally familiar with their lives. He examines the clean hole in the head. He treats himself to a glass of wine. He has doubts, he finds it hard to discover their sources. By examining himself in the mirror he can see his mood. By turning his face from the mirror he can see the bath. By turning from the bath he can see the towel rack. By turning from the towel rack he can see the toilet bowl. By turning from the toilet bowl he has made a complete circle and is back staring into the mirror. It's somebody about whom he has doubts, he has discovered in one complete revolution. By marching out of the bathroom he will leave the image behind him in the mirror and by leaving it behind he is free. Who is he now? He has doubts.

IV

He has doubts. He chews upon the stump of his cigar, he can express himself but to what end? Language is not the solution. He can join the rigid aggregate community but in what posture? He could make love to himself but with what thoughts? He could warm himself by the fire in winter, cool himself in the sea in summer. He could eat when hungry. He could cry when in pain, he could laugh when amused, he could think when in trouble. He is an ordinary man.

V

He is an ordinary man, he wants his breakfast, he needs his unhappiness, he wishes to be himself, he desires apotheosis as he is and so he shoots himself to relieve himself of his doubts. Brought to consciousness by this act, he dies. The man with the clean hole through his skull does not know the ordinary man is dead and the aggregate community never cares to change from its transfixed postures while he, lying dead, is studying that compelling emptiness in him beneath his breastbone and does not know how either to fill it or extract it to give him peace. He yearns to leap up from the floor to become a whirling dancer, an ecstatic, for the hell of it.

VI

For the hell of it he tries but lies still. He then knows he is dead and would inform the world. His body will, he decides. It is the evidence and his silence the message, and now what does life have to offer? It is time to think. He thinks, the earth has the answer that it presses upon him where he lies. It is not to think, he can be a stone or a cycle of existence, inside the cycle the air of emptiness, a small hole for a small life such as he had seen in the skull of the risen one. He can be a stone with a hole in it and he will always be the same. He has his comfort, he is ready to die success-fully, he dies and is complete, an ordinary man.

When I see fish swimming in water
I ask if I may join, I'm very sad
that we must stay apart
in this only world we have
between us. I see looks exchanged
among men and women, lips to bodies,
and when they part, I think
I am surrounded by a loud wailing
in the air. I raise my voice
in grief too, my one identity
with others.

R 3